# Best Venison Recipes

## Volume 1

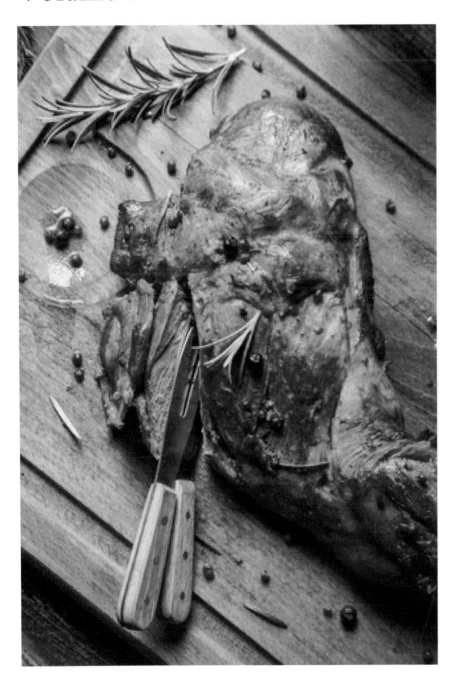

By Diana Loera

As with any food recipes, please check with your guests for food allergies before serving any recipe.

Please read through a recipe before beginning it.

Please do not let children attempt to make recipes.

Please check with your guests regarding food allergies before preparing any recipe.

Please remember cooking times may vary due to your oven.

**Other books by Diana Loera /Loera Publishing LLC**

Party Time Chicken Wings Favorite Recipes & Bonus Dip Recipes

Summertime Sangria

12 Extra Special Summertime Dessert Fondue Recipes

14 Extra Special Winter Holidays Fondue Recipes

Awesome Thanksgiving Leftover Revive Guide

What is the Paleo Diet & Paleo Diet Sampler

Stop Hot Flashes Now

Fast Start Guide to Flea Market Selling

USA Based Wholesale Directory 2012 Edition

USA Based Wholesale Directory 2013 Edition

USA Based Wholesale Directory 2014 Edition

Fast Start Guide to Flea Market Selling

I601A Our Journey to Ciudad Juarez

Meet Me at the County Fair – Mouthwatering Fair Food Recipes

Please visit www.LoeraPublishingLLC.com

You're also invited to follow me on Pinterest  www.Pinterest.com/Loera

## Table of Contents

## About the Creation of This Book

My brother, Christopher, has been an avid hunter through all of his boyhood and now adulthood. His almost grown son now follows in his hunting footsteps.

My brother often travels to hunt outside the rural Indiana location where he has lived his entire life. Over the years he and his wife have served venison a variety of ways and also made homemade jerky.

As I think you'll agree, our economy has changed drastically the past twenty years. You may hunt deer and cook recipes using it as you enjoy hunting and the deer meat is a nice treat. Or- you may be one of a growing group of people who are looking for ways to stretch every cent of their budget and the deer in the freezer is a must to survive the winter.

With that in mind, I selected a variety of recipes for venison. I also added in a couple recipes for jerky.

I'll be the first to tell you- I am a picky eater. The recipes in this book include many that I think will impress even the fussiest (aka pickiest eater).

Some of the recipes are fun family night meals and others are meals sure to impress your guests as they will think you hired a professional chef. Regardless, all the recipes are first class dishes compiled to give you a variety of choices for venison preparation.

There seems to be two opinions regarding what venison is- some people say it includes elk and antelope and some say it is only deer.

In this book, while all recipes are using deer, we can substitute elk, antelope and also beef in place of deer meat.

I hope you enjoy these recipes as much as I enjoyed selecting them for you.

I have included some color photos but in order to keep the book cost down, there is not an abundance of photos.

I did want to include at least some photos as readers of my other recipe books have commented that they appreciated that I includes photos.

Thank you for buying this book.

A portion of the profits from sales of this book will be donated to the Wounded Warriors Project.

http://www.woundedwarriorproject.org

**About Me**

Indiana farm raised, I grew up with a younger brother who hunted frequently. It was common to enjoy wild game weekly and I have many find memories of doing so.

As an adult, I've traveled frequently as I have owned and operated a media agency for many years. A couple years ago I began writing books and now am a full time author.

I enjoy looking for book topics that I think people may be interested in.

The idea for this book came to mind over three years ago and I was glad to finally see the collection of recipes grow so that I could create this book for you.

I enjoy trying new recipes and will soon publish a couple more recipe books. I enjoy wild game, especially quail and pheasant but venison is versatile and I wanted to publish a book showing the versatility from casual family night dining to impress the boss dishes. As you'll see, this book contains around 75 recipes. I still have more venison recipes to share and hope to soon create Volume 2.

I live in the Midwest with my husband, our Husky mix dog and a few cats.

Thank you again for reading my book.

## Venison Gyros

3 lbs. venison, cut into 1/4 thick strips

2 tablespoons olive oil

1 1/2 tablespoons ground cumin

1 tablespoon minced garlic

2 teaspoons dried marjoram

2 teaspoons ground dried rosemary

1 tablespoon dried oregano

1 tablespoon red wine vinegar

Salt and pepper to taste

1 Onion sliced

2 Tomatoes sliced

16 ounces Cucumber sauce (you can buy this premade at most larger grocery stores or ethnic grocers)

1 (12 ounce) package pita bread, warmed

Whisk together the olive oil, cumin, garlic, marjoram, rosemary, oregano, red wine vinegar, salt, and pepper in a large glass or ceramic bowl.

Add the venison strips, and toss to evenly coat.

Cover the bowl with plastic wrap, and marinate in the refrigerator at least 2 hours.

Heat a large skillet over medium-high heat.  Add venison strips and cook about a half lb.at a time.   Cook the venison strips until the venison has browned on the outside and is no longer pink on the inside, about 8 minutes. Pile the meat onto warmed pitas.

Top with sliced onion and tomato.

Add cucumber sauce and serve.

## Big Game Vegetable Soup

2 large shanks (or roast) of venison or beef

1 lb. baby carrots

1 cup onions, diced

4 potatoes, diced

Salt and pepper

1 large can tomatoes

1 tablespoon chopped garlic

Preheat oven to 375

Place meat in oven roaster, cover with water and bake until tender at 375°F.

Remove meat, cut pieces into smaller chunks and place in kettle on stovetop with all vegetables and seasoning. Add juice from roaster to pot.

Cover and cook until vegetables are done. Usually about 2 hours. You may have to add additional water depending on how much evaporates.

## Venison Crock Pot Chili

2 lbs. venison roast

1 packet of your favorite chili seasoning

2 tsp. chili powder

1 tsp. garlic powder

1 tsp. cumin

1 large onion, chopped

1 green pepper chopped

2- 15 oz. cans black beans, drained

2- 14½ oz. cans chili-style chopped tomatoes with juice

1 6 oz. can tomato paste

Salt and pepper, to taste

Optional- chopped jalapeno

Sour cream

1 bunch green onions, sliced

1 cup shredded Colby jack cheese

Cut the venison into 1-inch cubes.

Sauté onion and pepper along with venison cubes until nicely browned

Put the crock pot on low and place venison, chili seasoning, chili powder, garlic powder, and cumin.

Add in chopped onion, beans, tomato paste and 2 cans of chopped tomatoes.

Cover and cook for 8-10 hours.

Add salt and pepper to taste.

Serve at once, garnish with sour cream, green onions and cheese.

## Poblano Rubbed Venison Steaks with Cilantro& Lime Butter

4 (8-10 ounces each) venison steaks

1/2 cup butter, softened

1 tablespoon lime juice

1 tablespoon chopped fresh cilantro

2 tablespoons steak seasoning

1 tablespoon ancho chili powder (dried poblano peppers)

Whip together the butter, lime juice, and cilantro in a small bowl until well combined. Transfer the butter mixture onto a large piece of plastic wrap, gently wrap and form the butter into a log. Freeze until ready to use.

Prepare a grill for medium-high heat.

Mix together the steak seasoning and ancho chili powder in a small bowl. Rub the seasoning blend onto both sides of the venison steaks.

Grill the steaks to preferred doneness, 5 to 8 minutes per side for medium. Top each steak with a slice of the lime-cilantro butter to serve.

Note- we have several Mexican grocery stores in the area. I've found the quality of their peppers (and other produce) is superior to that of the big box grocery stores. The price for cilantro and peppers is also often considerably less at the Mexican grocers.

## Blue Cheese Venison Meat Loaf

1½ lb. ground venison

1 egg

¼ to ½ cup crumbled blue cheese

¼ cup onion, chopped

¼ cup milk

½ tsp. mustard, dry

¼ tsp. dried sage

¼ to ½ cup A1 steak sauce

½ cup bread crumbs

1/8 tsp. garlic powder

1 Tablespoon Worcestershire sauce

Salt and pepper to taste

1 Bag Instant Mashed Potatoes (Any flavor. I usually use Garlic or Loaded)

Bacon; Crisp & Crumbled

Heat the oven to 350 degrees F.

Mix half of the cheese and all the ingredients together.

Spread the venison mixture into an ungreased loaf pan, 9 X 5 X 3-inches or shape into a loaf in an ungreased baking pan.

Bake, uncovered, for 1 to 1 1/4 hours or until done. Drain off the excess fat.

Prepare the potatoes as directed on the package and stir in the remaining cheese. Spread the potatoes on the sides and top of the meat loaf. Sprinkle with the crumbled bacon and bake for an additional 10 minutes, or until the potatoes are lightly browned. Serve hot.

## Venison Breakfast Sausage

6 pounds ground venison

2 pounds ground pork

1/4 cup sugar-based curing mixture (such as Morton® Tender Quick®)

1 tablespoon fresh-ground black pepper

1 tablespoon crushed red pepper flakes

1/4 cup packed brown sugar

3 tablespoons dried sage

DIRECTIONS:

In a large bowl, sprinkle the venison and pork with the curing mixture, pepper, pepper flakes, sugar, and sage.

Mix very well.

Tip-When working with large quantities of sausage, cook a small piece to make sure the seasoning is exactly how you like it.

Divide into portions, place in freezer safe bags and freeze.

NOTE do not thaw any meat, create a recipe like this one and then refreeze. This is for meat not previously frozen.

## Venison Shish Kebabs

5 lbs. venison, cut into cubes

1/3 cup soy sauce

2-3/4 teaspoons white sugar

1 teaspoon ground ginger

1 teaspoon dry mustard powder

2-3/4 teaspoons garlic powder

1/2 teaspoon cayenne pepper

1/4 cup and 3 tablespoons vegetable oil

4 onions, cut into large chunks

7 jalapeno peppers, stemmed and cut in half

3 green bell peppers, cut in large chunks

32 Cherry tomatoes

Shish Kebab skewers 15-20

Whisk the soy sauce, sugar, ginger, mustard powder, garlic powder, and cayenne pepper in a large bowl until the sugar has dissolved.

Whisk in the vegetable oil, then stir in the venison cubes until evenly covered in the marinade. Cover the bowl with plastic wrap, and marinate in the refrigerator at least 4 hours. Place the wooden skewers into water to soak.

Preheat an outdoor grill for medium heat.

While the grill is heating, remove the venison from the marinade, and squeeze off excess. Discard the remaining marinade. Thread the venison cubes onto the skewers, alternating with the onion, jalapeno, tomatoes and bell pepper.

Cook the shish kabobs on the preheated grill, turning occasionally until cooked to your desired degree of doneness, about 10 minutes total for medium-rare.

## Crock Pot Venison Roast with Apples & Onions

1-1/2 teaspoons olive oil (plus a little additional for sautéing)

2 lbs. pounds boneless venison roast

2 large apples, cored and quartered

1 onion, sliced

1 clove crushed garlic

1 cup boiling water

1 cube beef bouillon


Dissolve the bouillon cube in hot water. Stir in olive oil.

Sauté the apples, garlic, onions and meat in pan with a little olive oil until nicely brown.

Transfer to crock pot on Low temperature.  Pour liquid mixture over and cover.

Cook until the roast is tender, about 6 to 8 hours.

If I'm home, I'll place crock pot on Medium High for first hour and then turn down to Low. I do check the pot every few minutes as I don't want the food to scorch.  If I'm not going to be in the house, I set the crockpot on Low.

Some crock pots have timers allowing you to change the temperature settings, I don't have one like that so I make do with the arrangement above.

## Broiled Venison Cubes

1 lb. Venison cubed in 1-2 inch size cubes depending on your personal preference

¼ cup Extra Virgin Olive Oil

2 cloves garlic, finely minced

½ cup grated Romano cheese

1 ½ cup dry bread crumbs

1 tablespoon dried cilantro

1 teaspoon sweet Hungarian paprika

¼ cup fresh diced parsley (use dried if necessary)

Salt and pepper


Preheat the broiler and set the oven rack about six inches from the heat source.

Put olive oil and garlic in a small saucepan and stir over medium low heat, removing before the garlic browns.

In a small bowl, put bread crumbs, Romano cheese, cilantro, paprika, parsley, salt and pepper.

Allow the olive oil/garlic mix to cool slightly then add to the crumb mixture and stir well.

Press the venison cubes into the mixture and coat them well then place on a baking sheet that is either non-stick or coated with aluminum foil.

Broil for 5 – 7 minutes, turning several times, until the crumbs are golden brown and the meat is done.

Best Venison Recipes    Diana Loera   2014   All Rights Reserved

## Venison with Butternut Squash, Pasta, and Kale

1 lb. ground venison

2 – 3 cups butternut squash, cubed and peeled (about ½-inch cubes)

1 1/2 tsp. olive oil

Salt and pepper

8 ounces of dry pasta, such as bowties or corkscrews

2 cups chopped kale (coarse middle stem removed)

2 slices bacon, chopped up

1 medium onion, chopped coarsely

2 cloves garlic, minced

Salt and pepper

1/2 cup beef broth

1 tablespoon honey

Dash of hot pepper sauce

Serve with shredded cheese, your favorite kind


Preheat oven to 400 degrees.

Mix the squash and olive oil in a large bowl; add salt and pepper and toss well.

Put the squash on a non-stick baking pan and bake for about 30 minutes until tender.

Set aside to cool.

Cook the bacon in a large covered skillet until crisp and add the venison and onion, stirring and cooking until browned and well-crumbled.

Add garlic and stir for one minute.

Add salt, pepper, broth, honey and hot pepper sauce.

Meanwhile, cook the pasta until al dente, adding the kale for the last minute or two.

Drain the pasta and add to the mixture in the skillet.

Add the cooked squash, cover and simmer for a minute or two, stirring occasionally, until squash is heated through and all ingredients are well blended.

Serve with a dish of grated cheese to sprinkle over the mixture.

## Venison Baked Spaghetti

INGREDIENTS:

1 lb. venison, cubed

1 (8 ounce) package angel hair pasta

2 tablespoons olive oil

1 Onion, diced

1 Bell Pepper, diced

1 (6 ounce) can tomato paste

2 (15 ounce) cans tomato sauce

1 teaspoon garlic salt

1 1/2 teaspoons dried dill

1 1/2 teaspoons dried marjoram

1 1/2 teaspoons Italian seasoning

4 ounces shredded Mozzarella cheese

1/4 cup grated Parmesan cheese

DIRECTIONS:

Preheat oven to 350 degrees F.

Spray a casserole dish with cooking spray.

Bring a large pot of lightly salted water to a boil. Add spaghetti and cook as instructed on package until al dente; drain.

Meanwhile, heat olive oil in a large skillet over medium-high heat.

Add venison and cook until well browned, about 5 minutes.

Stir in onion and green pepper, continue cooking until softened, about 4 minutes.

Add tomato paste and tomato sauce, season with garlic salt, dill, marjoram, and Italian seasoning.

Bring to a boil, then reduce heat to medium, and simmer for 5 minutes.

Place drained pasta into prepared casserole dish and pour venison over the top.

Sprinkle a mix of the Mozzarella and Parmesan cheeses on top.

Bake in preheated oven until the cheese is bubbly and browned, about 25 minutes.

**Venison Cabbage Rolls**

1 Lb. ground venison

1 chopped onion

Garlic (to taste)

¼ - ½ tsp nutmeg

Salt and Pepper (to taste)

2 cups tomato sauce

Cooked brown or white rice

Cabbage leaves

Grated cheese

Parsley


Prior to cooking the meat and sauce, boil cabbage leaves for 2-3 minutes.

Cook venison until brown; mix in onions, nutmeg, salt, pepper, and garlic to taste.

Cook on stove until onions are cooked

Mix in rice and 1 cup of tomato sauce.

Create rolls by adding the meat and sauce into boiled cabbage leaves.

Return rolls to pan, pouring the rest of the tomato sauce on top.

Allow rolls to simmer for 20 minutes.

Serve, garnishing with optional parsley and grated cheese.

**Slow Cooked Deer Ribs**

INGREDIENTS:

5 to 6 lbs. venison ribs

1 cup apple cider vinegar

1 (12 fluid ounce) bottle dark beer

3 celery ribs, chopped

3 carrots, chopped

3 chopped red bell peppers

1 head garlic, peeled

1 chopped onion

2 tablespoons Cajun seasoning

Salt and pepper, to taste

DIRECTIONS:

Preheat oven to 200 degrees F (95 degrees C).

Pour vinegar and beer into a large roasting pan.

Add the celery, carrots, peppers, garlic, and onion.

Rub the venison ribs with Cajun seasoning, salt and pepper to taste.

Place ribs in roasting pan and cover with a tight fitting lid or aluminum foil.

Bake in preheated oven for 18 hours, or until the meat is falling off of the bone

Venison Ribs

**Crispy Bacon & Jalapeno Deer Wraps**

INGREDIENTS:

1 pound venison tenderloin

1/4 cup and 2 tablespoons zesty Italian dressing

24 slices bacon

1/2 cup cream cheese

24 slices pickled jalapeno peppers

1 teaspoon seasoning salt to taste

DIRECTIONS:

1Cut the venison tenderloin into 8 strips lengthwise. Toss with Italian dressing, and allow to marinate for 1 hour in the refrigerator.

Preheat a grill for medium heat.

To assemble the venison wraps, lay a strip of venison on top of a strip of bacon.

Place a teaspoon of cream cheese at one end, and top with a slice of jalapeno.

Roll up and secure with a skewer.

Repeat with remaining ingredients.

Season the wraps with desired amount of seasoning salt.

Grill for 10 minutes, then turn over, and continue cooking until the bacon is crisp.

Bacon, Venison and Jalapeno Wraps

## Venison Chili

1 pound dry kidney beans

1 pound ground venison

1 pound venison stew meat, in 1/2-inch chunks

2 Tbsp. oil

2 cloves garlic, minced

3 teaspoons chili powder

1 tsp. salt

½ tsp. pepper

28-ounce can tomatoes, diced

1 large onion, diced

1 green pepper, diced

1 large green chili pepper, diced

¼ tsp. cumin

2 tablespoons parsley, chopped

¼ cup masa flour or all-purpose flour


Rinse beans and place in a large soup kettle.

Add 2qts water and 2 tsp. salt; cover the pot and bring to a boil.

Boil gently for about 2 hours, until beans are tender.

Brown meat in a large skillet containing oil and garlic.

Add chili powder, salt and pepper.

Cover and sauté for an hour.

Drain the beans and add 1½ quarts of water, tomatoes, onion, peppers, cumin and parsley.

Simmer for an hour, then add meat mixture.

Stir masa flour into ½ cup water to form a paste and blend into chili to thicken.

Simmer for 30 to 60 minutes and serve.

This dish goes well with cornbread.

## Venison Medallions with Juniper and Orange

This is a bit more detailed of a recipe with ingredients that may be a little harder to find. If you are looking for a totally different recipe that is sure to impress, this one is worth making.

For butter

7 tablespoons Irish butter such as Kerrygold, softened*

1 tablespoon drained green peppercorns in brine, coarsely chopped

1 garlic clove, minced

1 teaspoon freshly squeezed orange juice

1 teaspoon honey

1/2 teaspoon kosher salt

For venison

1 cup olive oil

1 tablespoon plus 1 teaspoon orange zest (from 2 oranges)

4 sprigs fresh sage, minced

1 teaspoon freshly ground black pepper

16 juniper berries, crushed with the backside of a knife

16 (3 1/2-ounce) venison medallions (each about 1/2- to 3/4-inch thick)

*Available at specialty foods shops. If unavailable, substitute regular unsalted butter and add 1 additional teaspoon kosher salt.

Make butter:

In food processor, combine all ingredients and pulse until well combined. Transfer to large sheet of wax paper and roll into 5-inch-long log. Wrap in wax paper and refrigerate at least 1 hour to allow flavors to develop.

Make venison:

In large glass baking dish, whisk together olive oil, orange zest, sage, pepper, and juniper berries. Add venison medallions and turn to coat. Let stand at room temperature at least 1 hour, turning meat occasionally.

Over moderate heat, heat large heavy skillet until hot.

Add 4 venison medallions and cook until undersides are well browned, about 3 minutes.

Turn over and cook to desired doneness (thermometer inserted into center will register 120°F for medium-rare), about 2 to 3 minutes for medium-rare.

Transfer to platter and cover loosely with foil.

Repeat with remaining medallions, cooking 4 at a time.

Slice log of butter into 8 coins.

Divide medallions among 8 plates and top each serving with 1 coin.

Serve immediately.

**Venison Meatloaf**

INGREDIENTS:

1-1/4 pounds ground venison

1 tablespoon and 3/4 teaspoon brown sugar

10 saltine crackers, crumbled

1-1/4 egg, beaten

1/2 teaspoon spicy brown mustard

1/4 teaspoon dried cilantro

1/2 teaspoon garlic powder

1/2 teaspoon dried minced onion flakes

1/4 teaspoon ground thyme

1-1/4 dashes cinnamon

1-1/4 dashes paprika

3 tablespoons and 2-1/4 teaspoons

Ketchup to taste

1 tablespoon and 3/4 teaspoon brown

Sugar

DIRECTIONS:

1.      Preheat oven to 350 degrees F (175 degrees C).

2.      Mix together venison, 1 tablespoon brown sugar, crackers, and egg in a bowl. Season with mustard, cilantro, garlic powder, onion flakes, thyme, cinnamon, and paprika; mix well. Pat mixture into a 9x9-inch pan, or a loaf pan.

3.      Bake in preheated oven to an internal temperature of 160 degrees F (70 degrees C), about 40 minutes. Stir together the ketchup, with 1 tablespoon brown sugar. Spread on top of the meatloaf, and place back in the oven for 10 minutes more.

## Venison and Cheese Stuffed Shells in Tomato Sauce

1 lb. box jumbo shells

1 carton Ricotta cheese

8 oz. shredded Mozzarella cheese

½ c. Parmesan cheese

1 egg

1 tsp parsley

1 lb. venison

1 medium chopped onion

3 cloves minced garlic

32 oz. spaghetti sauce warmed on stove

Olive oil to prevent sticking


Cook shells as package directs; drain, rinse in cool water, toss with olive oil to prevent sticking, and set aside.

Brown venison with onion and garlic.

Mix in parmesan and ricotta cheeses, ½ cup of mozzarella, egg and parsley.

Fill cooked shells with mixture and put in greased 9"x13" pan.

Cover with spaghetti sauce and remaining Mozzarella cheese.

Cover and bake at 350°F for 35 to 45 minutes.

Uncover 5 minutes before removing from oven.

Serve with salad and warm Vienna or French bread.

**Venison Cheesy Sloppy Joes**

1½ pounds ground venison

½ of a small onion, diced

2 Tbsp. mustard

1 can chicken gumbo soup

Salt and pepper to taste

½ tsp chili powder

1 tsp sugar

¼ pound shredded cheddar (or other) cheese

½ cup ketchup


Fry the venison and onion.

Pour off excess grease and add mustard, ketchup, soup and spices.

Simmer 15 to 20 minutes until thick.

Stir in cheese until melted and serve on buns.


Quick version – brown venison and onion, drain

Mix in a Sloppy Joe sauce mix

Let simmer 20-30 minutes, stirring regularly

You can add in cheese as above.

With both recipes I like topping with cheese slices right before serving (Pepper Jack and Colby are my two favorites) versus using the shredded cheese.

If I have time, I toast the cheese topped slice opened faced in the oven.

**Caramelized Onions with Venison in a Raspberry Marinade**

INGREDIENTS:

3/4 cup and 3 tablespoons raspberry vinaigrette   (I like Marzetti's brand the best)

2 tablespoons and 1-1/2 teaspoons Maple syrup

2 tablespoons and 1-1/2 teaspoons soy sauce

2-1/2 pounds venison, cut into 1/2-inch strips

 2 tablespoons and 1-1/2 teaspoons unsalted butter

2 tablespoons and 1-1/2 teaspoons olive oil

3/4 cup and 3 tablespoons water

2-1/2 sweet onions, thinly sliced

1 tablespoon and 3/4 teaspoon minced garlic

Salt to taste

Pepper to taste

2 tablespoons and 1-1/2 teaspoons white sugar

1.	Whisk together the raspberry vinaigrette, maple syrup, and soy sauce in a large bowl. Stir in the venison until well coated, and set aside.

2.	Bring the butter, olive oil, water, onions, and garlic to a boil in a large skillet over medium-high heat. Cook and stir until the onions have caramelized to a deep, golden brown, 10 to 15 minutes. Once the onions have turned a deep golden brown, stir in the sugar, and cook 2 to 3 minutes more.

3.	Stir in the venison along with the marinade. Cook and stir until the venison is no longer pink in the center, about 5 minutes.

Best Venison Recipes    Diana Loera  2014   All Rights Reserved

**Cheesy Venison Toasts**

Ingredients:

1 pound ground venison

1 pound hot & spicy sausage (such as Bob Evans brand)

1 pound Velveeta cheese, cubed    (I like using the Mexican Velveeta for a little extra kick)

1 loaf cocktail rye bread or French bread sliced

Directions:

In large skillet brown the venison and sausage, drain.

Add cubed Velveeta and cook on low heat until melted.

Arrange cocktail rye slices on an ungreased baking sheet.

Spoon about 2 Tablespoons of meat and cheese mixture onto each rye slice.

Broil for about 5 minutes or until the bread is toasting and the mixture sets with a slight crust forming.

Serve warm.

**Venison Corn Bake**

1 lb. venison (browned and drained)

1 small onion

1 can cream of mushroom soup

1 can cream of chicken soup

1 small container of sour cream

1 16 oz. can corn (drained)

½ package of egg noodles (cooked and drained)

1 sleeve of Ritz crackers

Salt & pepper to taste

Mix all above ingredients in a large casserole dish; add crushed Ritz crackers (or topping of choice). Bake covered at 375°F for 45 minutes. Uncover 5 minutes before removing from oven.

**Venison Cottage Cheese Pie**

1- 9" unbaked pie crust

1 chopped onion

1 cup sliced mushrooms

1 lb. ground venison

¼ tsp. pepper

2 Tbsp. flour

3 Tbsp. ketchup

2 eggs, beaten

1 cup cottage cheese


Brown together onion, mushroom, and ground venison in a heavy skillet.

Drain any excess fat.

Add pepper, ketchup and flour to skillet and cook and stir for 3 to 5 minutes.

Place meat mixture into the pie crust lined pan.

Beat eggs and add cottage cheese.

Pour this mixture over meat in the pie pan.

Bake at 350°F for 30-40 minutes, or until filling is set, crust is golden, and topping is puffed.

**Venison Terrine with Apricot**

This pretty terrine dish makes an impressive starter served with a salad of bitter leaves drizzled with a walnut or hazelnut dressing.  This recipe does take quite a bit of time but if you want something truly different for a special meal, this one is worth considering.


3 oz. chopped dried apricots

3 tbsp. brandy

1 1/2 Lb. minced Venison (use diced venison)

3/4 Lb. minced belly of pork

1 tsp. freshly grated ginger

2 allspice berries, crushed

6 juniper berries, crushed

Salt and freshly ground black pepper

3 1/2 oz. red wine or port

2 tbsp. olive oil

About 10 strips of thinly cut Italian pancetta or bacon

1 egg, beaten

Fig (for garnish)


Mix the apricots with the brandy, cover and soak overnight.


Pass the venison through a mincer.

Mix together the venison, pork, fresh ginger, allspice, juniper berries, salt and pepper with the wine or port and the olive oil.

Cover and marinate overnight.

The next day, preheat the oven to 350 degrees. Line a standard size loaf pan (I use the disposable ones) with the pancetta or bacon, keeping 3-4 strips for the top.

Beat the egg into the marinated Venison, then use just under half to fill the base of the terrine, pushing a ½ inch ridge up all the sides of the terrine.

Spoon the apricots into the hollow created by the ridge, then carefully cover with the remaining meat mixture to encase the apricots completely.

Smooth over and cover with the rest of the pancetta or bacon, folding over any stray strips.

Cover with foil, place on a cookie sheet and bake in the oven for 1 1/2 - 2 hours or until a skewer inserted into the middle, comes out clean.

Remove from the oven and place a weight on top. Cool then chill.

Run a knife around the edge of the tin and turn out. Serve at room temperature with good crusty rolls or bread, gherkins and pickles, or with a small leafy salad.

Venison Terrine

## Country Fried Venison

Ingredients

¾ lb. to 1 lb. of venison chops/steaks (2-3 big or 4-5 small pieces)

8 oz. package of sliced baby Portobello mushrooms

1 medium sweet onion, chopped

1- 12-16 oz. can of either beef or mushroom gravy

1 Tbsp. of garlic, minced

¼ cup green onion, chopped

Salt, pepper and seasoning salt

½ cup flour

¼ cup cornstarch

4 Tbsp. of butter or margarine

Season venison chops (to taste) using your favorite seasoning salt.

Place flour, cornstarch, and touch of salt and pepper into large Ziploc bag.

Put venison chops individually into the bag, shake to coat well.

Once all chops are coated, remove from bag to a plate.

Press coating into chops then let sit at room temperature for at least 10 minutes to help the flour stick to the venison.

Preheat a large (16") skillet (cast iron is suggested) to med-high heat.   If you do not have a cast iron skillet you will also need a baking pan.

Preheat oven to 350°.

Melt butter in skillet.

Add onion and sauté until almost transparent.

Add package of sliced mushrooms.

Allow onions and mushrooms to caramelize.

Just before onions and mushrooms are finished add the minced garlic.

Once onions, mushrooms, and garlic are done remove to a plate.

With the skillet still at medium-high heat, melt 2 tablespoons of butter.

Place venison into melted butter and brown on each side.

This will sear in the juices, not cook the venison completely through.

Once browned, drain oil then return onions, mushrooms, and garlic mixture to the pan.

Also add in entire can of beef or mushroom gravy. Make sure chops are mostly covered.

Place the uncovered cast iron skillet in the oven for 10 minutes to finish the dish. Remember, if your skillet is not cast iron, you will need to move the mixture into a baking pan.

Remove from oven and serve.

**Coffee Grilled Venison**

1 pound of venison, in one or two chunks

1 tbsp. brown sugar

1 tsp. garlic powder

¼ tsp. ground ginger

½ tsp. onion powder

1 ½ tsp. instant coffee

½ tsp. salt

1/8 tsp. pepper

½ tsp. paprika


Dressing

½ cup light ranch dressing

1 tbsp. mayonnaise

1/4 tsp. dill weed

Fresh parsley (optional)

1 ½ tbsp. fresh lemon juice

1 tsp. Dijon mustard.


Mix together all the dry ingredients.

Score the venison in a diamond pattern, then rub the dry mix into both sides of the meat.

Place the venison in a stainless steel or other oven-proof skillet and brown on each side.

Preheat the oven to 475 degrees and once the venison is browned, put the skillet in the oven for about 5 minutes.

Remove from the heat and let rest for several minutes before cutting.

Check temperature for desired doneness, an internal temperature of about 140 is medium.

Slice into thin strips.

Serve with a dressing made from light ranch dressing, stirred together with dill weed, snipped fresh parsley if available, fresh lemon juice and Dijon mustard.

## Cherry Cream Cheese Venison Appetizer

1 16 oz. package of softened cream cheese

¼ cup chopped dry cherries

1 sleeve Ritz crackers

Sliced venison salami

Mix softened cream cheese and cherries in a bowl.

Place slice of venison salami on cracker and top with cream cheese/cherry mix.

If you want to up your presentation, use a pastry bag with a wider tip.

Then you can make a nice swirl dollop of the cream cheese and cherry mix.

You can also use chopped dried apricots instead of cherries.

**Seared Venison Fillet with Caramelized Plums**

This dish takes about an hour to make but is a beautiful autumn and winter dish. There are 3 components – the Venison Jus, the Venison Filets and the Caramelized Plums

Venison Jus

1 tbsp. canola oil
Venison trimmings
1 carrot, roughly chopped
2 stalks celery, roughly chopped
1 onion, peeled, roughly chopped
2 cups water
1 cup chicken stock
1 sprig thyme
1 handful parsley
6 black peppercorns
1/2 cup one third beef stock reduction
1/4 cup red wine

Caramelized Plums
4 Tablespoons unsalted butter
2 red plums, halved, stones removed (I've substituted can plums, if so omit the sugar below)
2 tbsp. sugar
Splash of white balsamic vinegar

Venison
2 lbs. Venison Fillet, trimmed
2 tbsp. olive oil
Salt and freshly ground black pepper

To make the venison jus, heat the canola oil in a large frying pan over high heat and sear the trimmings and bones until caramelized, ensuring the pan is scraped regularly.

Add the carrot, celery and onion and allow to cook for a minute.

Add the water, chicken stock, herbs and peppercorns.

Bring to the boil, reduce heat to a simmer and reduce the sauce by two thirds, then strain.

Add the beef jus and red wine and simmer until dark and slightly syrupy.

Season to taste and strain again.


To make the caramelized plums-

Heat the butter in a frying pan over medium heat.

Sprinkle the plums with sugar and place flat side down in the frying pan.

Cook for a few minutes until caramelized.

Reduce the heat and cook on low for a further 30 minutes.

Deglaze the frying pan with white balsamic vinegar, allow to reduce, then remove the plums from the pan and set aside.

To prepare the venison, brush the venison with olive oil and season well with salt and pepper.

Heat a little olive oil in a large frying pan over high heat.

Sear the venison on all sides until well browned; approximately 5 minutes in total.

Remove from the frying pan, cover with tin foil and allow to rest for 10 minutes.

To serve, slice the venison into thin slices.

Place the caramelized plums on a serving plate and top with the venison.

Serve the venison jus on the side.

Venison with Caramelized Plums

## Crescent Roll Venison Lasagna

2 packs of crescent rolls

1 ½ lb. Ground venison

1 onion (diced)

Garlic (to taste)

32 oz. Spaghetti sauce

16 oz. Ricotta cheese

16 oz. Italian cheese shredded

Cook ground venison with chopped onions and garlic to taste until it is fully browned.

Mix in spaghetti sauce just covering the meat, into a mixing bowl, set aside. Open crescent roll packages and arrange in a circle on a cookie sheet.

The crescent dough should be overlapping and the long part of the dough pieces should be pointing out with a circle in the middle (looks like a sun when you are finished).

Spoon the mixture onto the overlapping dough base, allowing enough dough to be folded over the filling to create a roll. Sprinkle ricotta and Italian cheeses on the venison.

Take the long part of the dough pieces and bring over the venison cheese and tuck the long part under the dough.

Do this with all the long ends. It should resemble a circle or ring when you are finished. There will also be space between the long ends where you can see the venison and cheese; this is the way it should be.

Bake in the oven at 375ºF for approximately 20 minutes, until it is golden brown.

Serve with more cheese sprinkled on top.

**Venison Crostini**

1 loaf of French bread, sliced

Small venison loin or tenderloin

1 Tbsp. olive oil

2 Tbsp. cracked black pepper

2 Tbsp. ginger powder

2 Tbsp. garlic powder

1 Tbsp. thyme powder

Roasted red or Poblano pepper (Ethnic aisle at grocery story will have in cans or jars)

Roasted red onion, sliced - optional

Boursin cheese (or your favorite sweet cheese spread)

1/8 cup melted butter

Salt

Balsamic vinegar reduction

Pre-heat the oven broiler to high or highest heat. Move the top rack as close as you safely can to cook loin.

Use some of the olive oil to rub over the venison. Mix together the cracked black pepper, ginger, garlic and thyme and rub onto venison to taste. Place venison on a baking sheet and cook/broil for 3 minutes.

Remove from heat, brush with butter and sprinkle salt on exposed side then flip loin and repeat process on the other side. Return to the broiler and cook until venison is just done.  Remove from oven and let the venison rest before slicing into thin pieces.

## Venison Egg & Cheese Soufflé

10 slices bread cubed (without crusts)

8 oz. Cheese- cheddar

6 eggs

3 cups milk

6 slices of bacon- fried and crumbled

½ tsp. Salt

Optional additions – sautéed mushrooms or sautéed peppers or sautéed onions – or all three if you'd like.

Place bread cubes in greased 9"x13" pan. Mix remaining ingredients; pour over bread. Let soak overnight.

Bake at 350°F for 45-50 minutes (cover for first 20 min) until set in center.

You can garnish with sesame seeds or a sprig of fresh basil or fresh rosemary for an added presentation touch.

**Venison Empanadas**

These tasty hand held little pies are fun to eat.  Great for Super Bowl parties too!  I usually serve a horseradish dip on the side for those who want a little more kick.   I've also added a few diced jalapenos but to make them versatile for parties, I would not add the jalapenos or make two batches and label the jalapeno ones as hot.

Filling:

1 lb. ground venison

1 large slice of white sandwich bread, torn into quarters

½ Cup plus 2 Tablespoons chicken broth

Salt and pepper

Oil

2 cups of onion, chopped fine

4 medium garlic cloves, minced

1 teaspoon cumin

¼ teaspoon cayenne

1/8 teaspoon ground cloves

1 bunch cilantro leaves, chopped

2 hard-cooked eggs, chopped

1/3 cup raisins, chopped

¼ cup green olives, chopped

4 teaspoons cider vinegar

Dough:

3 cups all -purpose flour

1 cup Masa Harina (substitute regular flour if unavailable)

1 Tablespoon sugar

2 teaspoons table salt

1 ½ sticks butter, cut into cubes

1 cup cold water


Oil for baking


Preheat oven and baking sheets (I used sheets with edges not the totally flat ones) at 425.

For dough:  Combine dry ingredients, cut butter into flour (pulse in food processer), sprinkle liquid onto mixture and combine until tacky.  Portion dough into 12 equal pieces and refrigerate.

For filling:  Process bread and 2 Tablespoons of chicken broth in food processor.  Add venison and salt/pepper to taste, pulsing until meat and bread paste is combined.  Sauté onions in oil, adding spices and garlic when onions are nearly opaque.  Add venison mixture and cook until meat is browned.  Add remaining chicken broth and simmer 5 minutes.  Transfer to a bowl, add remaining ingredients and allow mixture to cool.


Roll dough into rounds, place ½ cup filling on half of each round, fold closed and crimp edges.  Place 2 Tablespoons of oil into each preheated pan and allow to heat.  When oil is hot, place empanadas onto pan, brush with oil, and bake 25 to 30 minutes.

Venison Empanadas

## Old School Recipe Deer Jerky

This is an adaptation of the very first jerky recipe I made in the 80s. I used beef at that time but it works well with deer too. I have used a dehydrator and the oven method. I liked the dehydrator method but my dehydrator finally bit the dust and I have yet to replace it.

5 lb. Venison cut into ¼ inch thick slices

Marinade:

2 ounces of Liquid Smoke

¾ cup of Worcestershire sauce

¾ cup of soy sauce (low sodium is available)

1 tsp of seasoning salt

1 tsp of garlic powder

1 tsp of onion powder

1 tsp of pepper

Tabasco sauce (to taste)

Gallon size Zip Lock baggies


Mix Liquid Smoke, Worcestershire sauce, soy sauce, seasoning salt, garlic and onion powder, pepper and Tabasco sauce in a bowl.

Put sliced meat in baggies and pour marinade over. Let marinate overnight.

I put the baggies inside of bowls in my fridge in case a baggy leaks.

Remove meat from baggies and place meat in dehydrator or on foil lined baking sheet.

Dispose of leftover marinade and used baggies.

Place meat in dehydrator or oven at 125-140°F degrees for 10 to 12 hours.

Let cool and then store in unused baggies.

Venison Jerky

## Florentine Venison Lasagna

1 lb. venison

Onion, chopped

1 can cream of mushroom soup

½ cup shredded Swiss cheese

1 package lasagna noodles

Frozen spinach, thawed and drained

Fresh thyme

Sun-dried tomatoes


Cook the venison and onion in a skillet on stove. In a separate pan, mix together cream of mushroom soup and Swiss cheese. Cook until all of the cheese is melted.


Mix spinach, thyme, and sun-dried tomatoes in with the venison and onion along with half of the soup and cheese mixture.


Cut the lasagna noodles vertically in half. Line each noodle with the venison mixture. Roll each noodle and place in a greased 13 x 9 pan. Top each noodle with the remaining soup mixture. Cook at 350-degrees for about 25-30 minutes.

Venison Florentine Lasagna

**Venison Frittata**

2 Tbsp. vegetable oil

½ pound ground venison

Cajun seasoning to taste

8-ounces of mushrooms, chopped

Salt and freshly ground black pepper

½ cup onion, chopped

½ cup sweet red pepper

1 container egg substitute (such as Egg Beaters)

2 eggs

Green onion, diced

1 cup grated sharp Cheddar

Optional- sliced tomatoes and broccoli


Place the oil, venison and mushrooms in a large nonstick skillet.

Sprinkle with Cajun seasoning, salt and pepper and sauté until the venison has browned.

Add onions and red peppers and continue cooking until tender.

Whisk the egg substitute and the eggs in a bowl, then pour over the meat and vegetables. Stir gently.

Reduce the heat to low, cover the skillet and cook until eggs are set around the edges, about five minutes.

Top with sliced tomatoes and broccoli (optional)

Sprinkle with cheese and green onions and place under the broiler until cheese is melted and slightly browned.

Let the frittata stand for a couple minutes before slicing.

Venison Frittata with Tomatoes and Broccoli

## Venison Gravy (to serve over biscuits)

1 pound ground venison

1 can mushrooms (4-ounce)

1 can cream of mushroom soup

1 can milk

Salt and pepper to taste


Brown the venison in a large fry pan.

Add mushrooms and cook for a few minutes.

Add mushroom soup and milk; stir and cook until smooth and hot.

Salt and pepper to taste and serve over hot biscuits.

## Venison with Cranberry Wine Sauce

4 venison tenderloin steaks, about 1 inch thick (8 to 10 ounces each)

1/2 cup dry red wine or nonalcoholic red wine

1 tablespoon Dijon mustard

1/4 teaspoon salt

1/4 teaspoon coarsely ground pepper

1 tablespoon olive or vegetable oil

1/2 cup beef broth

1/2 cup dried cranberries

2 tablespoons currant or apple jelly

1 tablespoon butter or stick margarine

2 medium green onions, sliced (2 tablespoons)

Mix wine and mustard until well blended.

Place venison in a Ziploc plastic food-storage bag or shallow glass or plastic dish.

Pour wine mixture over venison; turn venison to coat with wine mixture.

Seal bag or cover dish and refrigerate 2 to 4 hours turning venison occasionally.

Remove venison from marinade; reserve marinade.

Sprinkle venison with salt and pepper. Heat oil in 12-inch nonstick skillet over medium-high heat.

Cook venison in oil about 4 minutes, turning once, until brown.

Add broth to skillet; reduce heat to low.

Cover and cook about 10 minutes, turning venison once, until venison is tender and desired doneness. Be careful not to overcook as you don't want tough, overcooked meat.

Remove venison from skillet; keep warm.

Stir marinade into skillet. Heat to boiling, scraping up any bits from bottom of skillet; reduce heat to medium.

Cook about 5 minutes until mixture is slightly reduced.

Stir in cranberries, jelly, butter and onions.

Cook 1 to 2 minutes, stirring occasionally, until butter is melted and mixture is hot.

Serve sauce with venison.

Venison with Cranberry Wine Sauce

## Greek Style Venison Steak

2 Venison steaks

¾ cup sour cream

1/3 - 1/2 cup of chopped cucumber

3 tablespoons crumbled feta cheese

2 tablespoons chopped Greek olives

Marinade:

½ cup steak sauce

1 tablespoon olive oil

2 tablespoons lemon juice

Mix marinade by adding steak sauce, olive oil, and lemon juice; marinate the steaks for approximately two hours. Save some of the marinade, that has not touched the raw meat, as a garnish.

Grill steaks for 10-12 minutes, until they are cooked through to prevent contamination. Mix the sour cream and cucumber and add on top of the finished steaks on the plate. Add feta cheese and olives as a garnish, enhancing its Greek taste.

## Grilled Venison Rolls

Venison steaks

Tooth picks soaked in water

Green onion

Asparagus spears


Marinade:

Soy sauce

Garlic

Lime juice

Sesame oil


Cut hind steaks along the grain creating thin pieces while still partially frozen. This allows ease in removing fat and cutting. Marinade steaks in soy sauce, garlic, lime juice, and sesame oil. Roll marinated steaks around a couple pieces of asparaguses and green onions respectively. Fix rolled steaks with moistened toothpicks to ensure them from not catching on fire. Place rolls onto grill, basting them with extra marinade ensuring good moistness and taste. Periodically roll the steaks as to cook all the way through. Venison steaks are done when they are completely brown all of the way through.

## Grilled Venison Steaks

Venison Steaks

½ cup Heinz 57 Sauce

¼ cup honey

Garlic salt

Black pepper


Season venison steaks with garlic salt and black pepper (to taste). Mix ½ cup Heinz 57 sauce with ¼ cup honey. Spread over both sides of steak. Broil at 425°F for approximately 20 minutes (or until prepared to your liking). Turn once and brush with sauce again. You can also heat leftover sauce to serve at the table.

## Golden Venison Supreme

1 pound venison tenderloin

2 cans Campbell's golden mushroom soup

1 egg, beaten

1 cup milk

1 tsp. garlic salt

1 tsp. pepper

1 cup of flour

1 stick butter

1 cup olive oil

1 cup water

After removing all fat and tendons, cut venison into slices (across grain) and soak in several rinses of fresh water.

Drain venison and place (or dip) in mixture of milk, egg, garlic salt, and pepper for 15-20 minutes. Heat butter and oil in a large skillet.

Drain venison (but do not wash) and place in bag with flour.

Shake to coat venison and fry pieces in skillet to a golden brown coating on both sides.

Preheat oven to 375°F. Place venison pieces flat (one layer thick) in a glass oven pan.

Mix soup with pan drippings and cover venison.

Add water, cover and bake 1 hour. Serve with mashed potatoes or rice.

## Hash Brown Potato Venison Loaf

1½ cups refrigerated shredded hash brown potatoes

1 onion, chopped

2 cloves garlic, minced

1 Tbsp. olive oil

3 eggs, lightly beaten

2/3 cup Italian flavored dry bread crumbs

1/3 cup barbecue sauce

1 tsp. salt

¼ tsp. pepper

1½ lbs. ground venison

Preheat oven to 375°F. Place potatoes in a large bowl and set aside.

In heavy skillet over medium heat, sauté onion and garlic in olive oil until tender, about 5 minutes.

Add to potatoes along with eggs, bread crumbs, 1/3 cup of the barbecue sauce, salt and pepper and mix well, until thoroughly combined.

Add ground venison and mix gently, just until combined.

 Shape meatloaf mixture into an 8"x 4" loaf.

I prefer to put the loaf on a wire rack inside a baking pan

Bake at 375°F for 70-75 minutes or until center is no longer pink and instant read thermometer reads 160°F when inserted in center of loaf. Let stand, covered, 15 minutes before slicing.

## Hash Brown Venison Quiche

5 cups frozen loose-packed shredded potatoes, thawed

¼ cup butter, melted

1 cup cooked ground venison

1 cup shredded cheddar cheese

¼ cup green onion, chopped

3 eggs

¾ cup milk

½ tsp. salt

½ tsp. pepper


Press the hash browns between paper towels to remove excess moisture then press them into the bottom and up the sides of an ungreased 9-inch pie plate.

Drizzle with butter.

Bake at 425°F for 25 minutes.

Combine the venison, cheese, and onion; spoon over the crust.

In a small bowl, beat the eggs, milk, salt and pepper.

Pour over all.

Reduce heat to 350°F; bake for 25 to 30 minutes or until a knife inserted near the center comes out clean.

Allow to stand for 10 minutes before cutting.

**Mustard and Herb Crusted Venison Medallions**

This is a delicious recipe but please ensure your guests do not have nut allergies before preparing this recipe.

1 ½ pounds venison loin, cut into thin medallions

½ cup Dijon mustard

1 cup chopped toasted walnuts

1 cup chopped toasted pecans

½ cup breadcrumbs

1 teaspoon salt

1 teaspoon cumin

1 teaspoon sugar

1 teaspoon dried thyme

½ teaspoon black pepper

3 tablespoons olive oil


Directions:

Smother medallions on both sides in mustard. Set aside.

In a medium bowl, combine nuts, breadcrumbs, and spices.

Dredge medallions in mixture, shaking off excess.

Heat oil in a large skillet over medium-high.

Add medallions and cook until browned on both sides, about 10 minutes total.

Serve immediately.

## Horseradish Crusted Venison Tenderloin

1 venison tenderloin

Kosher salt

3 Tbsp. Italian style bread crumbs

1 Tbsp. plus 2 teaspoons vegetable oil

1¼ tsp. ground black pepper

1½ Tbsp. minced shallot

2 Tbsp. minced or pressed garlic

¼ cup well-drained prepared horseradish

2 Tbsp. minced fresh parsley

½ tsp. minced fresh thyme

6 ounces coarsely-crushed potato chips

1½ tsp. mayonnaise

1½ tsp. Dijon mustard

½ tsp. unflavored powdered gelatin

Sprinkle roast with kosher salt.

Cover with plastic wrap, and let stand at room temperature for one hour.

Adjust oven rack to middle position and heat oven to 400°F.

Toss bread crumbs with 2 tsp oil, ¼ tsp salt, and ¼ tsp pepper in a non-stick skillet.

Cook over medium heat, stirring frequently, until golden brown.

Cool on rimmed baking sheet then toss with shallot, garlic 2 Tbsp. horseradish, parsley, thyme and crushed potato chips.

Pat tenderloin dry with paper towels and sprinkle evenly with remaining teaspoon of pepper.

Heat one tablespoon of oil in non-stick skillet over medium-high heat until just smoking. Sear tenderloin until well browned on all sides.

Transfer to wire rack and let rest 10 minutes.

Combine remaining 2 Tbsp. of horseradish, mayonnaise and mustard in a small bowl.

Just before coating tenderloin with paste, add gelatin and combine.

Spread horseradish paste over top and sides of meat, leaving bottom and ends bare.

Roll coated sides of tenderloin in bread-crumb mixture, pressing gently so crumbs just cover the paste; pat off any excess.

Return tenderloin to wire rack and place on rimmed cookie sheet.

Roast until thermometer registers 120°F for medium rare.

Transfer roast to carving board and let rest 20 minutes (the venison will continue to cook during that time).

Carefully cut the meat crosswise into ½-inch thick slices and serve with horseradish cream sauce.


Horseradish Cream Sauce:

½ cup heavy cream

½ cup horseradish

1 tsp salt

1/8 tsp cracked black pepper

Whisk until cream just thickens. Gently fold in horseradish, salt and pepper – refrigerate at least 30 minute prior to serving.

## Hot & Sweet Jerky

This is a twist on traditional jerky as you are grinding the meat. To me it is a bit more like Slim Jim type sticks than what I would consider jerky but it is still tasty.

10 pounds deer meat

2 cups chopped fine onions

2 cups brown sugar

1 cup red wine vinegar

1 cup ketchup

4 quarts cold water

2 tsp. Mesquite smoke flavor

3 tsp. curing salt

2 tsp. garlic powder

9 Tbsp. salt

2 Tbsp. chili powder

3 Tbsp. black pepper

3 Tbsp. cayenne pepper

2 Tbsp. ground yellow mustard seed

Grind the meat. Mix all other ingredients and then stir them into the ground venison.

Using a jerky shooter, form strips of meat on the shelves of a food dehydrator. It will depend on the type o dehydrator that you have but remember this is a bit different than traditional "flat" jerky so you may need to allow extra time.

The other option is to cook in the oven at 125-140 degrees for 10 to 12 hours – again, you may need to allow extra time.

Remove from heat source, let cool and store in freezer bags.

The recipe we followed said store in freezer but we have stored in refrigerator also.

## Huevos Rancheros with Venison Chile Sauce

½ lb. ground venison

2 tbsp. finely chopped onion

1 16oz can of tomatoes, drained

2 to 4 drops Tabasco sauce or hot sauce

1 tsp. salt

1 can of mild chili beans, drained

4 eggs

Soft corn tortillas

Olive oil

Shredded Cheese (Monterey Jack, Cheddar, or Mexican blend)

Sour Cream

Avocado slices


Cook onion and venison until brown.

Add the can of drained tomatoes, Tabasco/hot sauce, and salt.

Cook for one to two more minutes.

Add chili beans.

Turn heat to low and simmer sauce for 10 minutes.


While sauce is simmering, in a separate skillet heat 2 tbsp. olive oil to medium heat.

Add corn tortillas one at a time, flipping after 30 seconds to cook both sides.

Place two tortillas on each plate.

Using the same skillet, fry eggs on one side in remaining olive oil until egg whites are mostly cooked through, but yolks are still slightly runny.

Place each egg on cooked tortillas.

Layer tortillas and eggs with chili sauce (chili sauce will finish "cooking" the tops of the eggs).

Garnish with cheese, sour cream and avocado slices.

## Hunter's Style Venison

1½ pounds of venison, cut in chunks (need not be the most tender portions)

¼ cup butter or margarine

1 pound sliced mushrooms

1 bunch of green onions, chopped

1 can beef bouillon

½ cup dry white wine

Parsley

Onion powder

Garlic powder

Herb croutons


Brown the venison in butter or margarine, add mushrooms and green onions and sauté for several minutes. Add bouillon, seasonings and wine, cover and simmer for two hours, until meat is very tender, or remove to a baking dish, cover and bake at 325°F for two hours. When ready to serve, add 2 cups herb croutons, stir and serve.

## Venison Lasagna

¾ lb. of venison

¼ lb. of ground beef

½ cup of chopped onion

1 - 2 cloves of garlic

1 - 7 ½ ounce can of tomatoes, cut up

1 - 28 ounce can of tomato sauce

1 - 12 ounce can of tomato paste

2 teaspoons of dried basil, crushed

2 teaspoons of dried oregano, crushed

½ teaspoon of salt

½ teaspoon of pepper

1 box of lasagna noodles

1 beaten egg

2 cups of ricotta cheese

½ cup of parmesan cheese

1 tablespoon of parsley flakes

1 - 4 cup bag of shredded mozzarella cheese

Heat oven to 375°F.

For meat sauce, brown venison, beef and onions.

Add garlic to meat and simmer until meat is brown and onion is tender.

Drain fat.

Stir in the tomato sauce and paste and then add the basil and oregano.

If desired, add the salt and pepper.

Bring to a boil and then simmer for 15 minutes.

Meanwhile, cook the lasagna noodles according to the package directions and drain.

For filling, add the beaten egg to the ricotta cheese and ¼ cup of the parmesan cheese and the parsley.

Gently fold together.

Layer half of the cooled noodles in the bottom of a 12 x 7½ x 2-inch baking dish.

Spread with half of the ricotta cheese filling.

Top with half of the venison meat sauce and then half of the mozzarella cheese.

Repeat the entire process.

Sprinkle the remaining parmesan cheese on top.

Bake in a 375°F oven for 45 to 60 minutes or until heated through.

**Venison Lettuce Wraps**

Romaine lettuce leaves

1 pound ground venison

1 large onion, chopped

2 tablespoons minced garlic

1 tablespoon reduced-sodium soy sauce

1/4 cup hoisin sauce2 teaspoons minced fresh ginger

1 tablespoon rice wine vinegar or red wine vinegar

2 teaspoons sweet Asian chili pepper sauce

1 can (8 ounce size) sliced water chestnuts or bamboo shoots, drained, finely chopped

1 bunch green onions, thinly sliced

2 teaspoons Asian sesame oil


Rinse lettuce leaves, keeping them whole. Set aside to drain.


Cook venison in a large skillet over medium heat, stirring often to break up the meat. Add onion, garlic, soy sauce, hoisin sauce, ginger, vinegar and chili sauce. Cook until the meat is crumbled and brown. Add water chestnuts or bamboo shoots and green onions. Cook until onions begin to wilt, about 2 minutes.


Stir in sesame oil. Arrange lettuce leaves on the outer edge of a platter. Spoon meat mixture into center of the lettuce leaves and eat like a taco.

**Traditional Jerky**

1/2 cup brown sugar

1 tbsp. Soy sauce

2 tbsp. Worcestershire Sauce

2 tbsp. Liquid Smoke

1 tbsp. Salt

2-1/2 tbsp. Garlic Powder

1 tbsp. Onion Powder

1-2 tbsp. of Black pepper, 2 will make it pretty spicy.

Mix all ingredients, and add water sparingly – up to ¼ cup maximum.

Place meat in a glad or plastic bowl with a lid.

Pour marinade over meat and stir gently to ensure all meat is covered.

Allow meat to soak in the marinade for at least 12 hours.

Remove meat from marinade and either use a dehydrator based on the instructions for the dehydrator or you can use the traditional oven method:

Place jerky strips on a slotted baking pan and place the slotted pan on a cookie sheet. Put the oven temp at 125-140°F degrees for 10 to 12 hours.

Remove from oven or dehydrator and let cool. Then bag in to Zip Lock (or other similar brand baggies). Store in fridge up to 3 weeks.

**Mesquite Venison Jerky Recipe**

Ingredients

1 pound venison steak, cut into 1/4 inch strips

1 cup soy sauce

1/2 cup packed brown sugar

2 tablespoons Mesquite flavored liquid smoke concentrate

1 tablespoon ground paprika

3 cloves garlic minced

1/4 teaspoon salt

Add all of the ingredients together in a large bowl and add in the venison steak.

Marinate the venison for 12-24 hours.

Follow the directions on your dehydrator or use the traditional oven method of setting your oven at 125-140°F degrees for 10 to 12 hours.

Remove finished jerky from heat source and allow to cool.  Place in air tight baggies and store in fridge up to 3 weeks.

## Lucky 7 Hot & Sweet Jerky

7 lbs. Venison

1 Bottle of KC Masterpiece Honey Teriyaki Marinade

1 ½ Cups Brown Sugar (loosely packed)

1 ½ Cups Worcestershire Sauce

1 1 /2 Cups Soy Sauce (you can use the low sodium kind)

1 Cup Teriyaki Sauce

1 tsp. Habanero Sauce (Start with ¼ or ½ teaspoon if you aren't sure about the level of heat)

Hot Sauce (as per your level of heat – the habanero may be enough.

1 tsp Freshly Ground Black Pepper

1 tsp Garlic Powder (NOT Garlic Salt)

1 tsp. Seasoned Salt

1 tsp Garlic powder

1 tsp Liquid Smoke

Optional – Cayenne Pepper

I suggest using a gallon size baggy for the marinade.  This marinade may stain your plastic bowls so mixing it in a baggy eliminates that potential problem.

Break the recipe down into several bags.

Add meat to the bags.

Ensure the meat is nicely covered and then place the bags inside bowls inside the fridge.

Ideally the meat will marinade for 24-48 hours.

I suggest using all "hot" ingredients sparingly and tasting the marinade before using it. If you start with less, you can always increase the heat.

Move the marinating meat around in the baggies a couple times during the day if possible.

After 24-48 hours remove meat from the baggies and either use your dehydrator or the traditional oven method to make jerky.

Discard the leftover marinade.

**Smoky Venison Jerky**

2 pounds sliced venison

1/4 cups soy sauce

1-2 Tbsp. Worcestershire sauce

1/2 tsp Morton Tender Quick Cure

1/2 tsp black pepper

1/2 tsp garlic powder

1/2 tsp onion powder

1/4 tsp seasoned salt

2 Tbsp. brown sugar

2 Tbsp. Liquid Smoke

Mix all ingredients (except venison) and stir until sugar is completely dissolved.

Put venison in a lidded bowl.  Pour marinade over meat and gently stir to ensure meat is covered.

Cover bowl.

Let marinate overnight in fridge.

Remove meat from bowl the next day and discard leftover marinade.

Use either your dehydrator or traditional oven method to make the jerky.

**Hearty Venison Soup**

1 lb. ground venison

1 lb. Italian sausage

2 tablespoons minced garlic

1/3 cup chopped onion, sautéed

Salt and pepper to taste

Crushed red pepper

1 cup water

1 large can of chicken broth

1 bag of chunked frozen potatoes

1 small bag mini carrots

1 ½ cups chopped green onion

½ cup fresh parsley

Brown Venison in a pot and add Italian sausage. Ensure both meats are thoroughly cooked and then add remaining ingredients above to the pot

Mix ingredients in a large pot and allow it to simmer for 60 minutes.

Serve with cornbread, French bread or warm rolls.

## Venison Meatballs

1 pound ground venison

2/3 cup bread crumbs

1/3 cup Parmesan cheese

2 tsp. dried parsley

1 tsp. garlic powder

1/3 cup milk

2 eggs

Salt and pepper to taste

1 jar spaghetti sauce (see below)

In a large mixing bowl, beat eggs with milk. Add bread crumbs, Parmesan cheese, parsley, and garlic powder; mix well. Add ground meat and knead with your hands until well blended. Form into meatballs about the size of golf balls.

Brown the meatballs on all sides.

If you are serving with pasta or on French bread then put the meatballs in a pot of spaghetti sauce and simmer, covered, for an hour.

If placing on French bread, put some of the spaghetti sauce on the bread, add meatballs, a bit more sauce and top with mozzarella cheese. Place on cookie sheet in oven heated to 350 F until cheese melts.

If serving with other dishes, you can serve the meatballs with potatoes, mac and cheese or countless other dishes. I like the versatility of the meatballs as you have numerous options.

Venison Meatballs with Potatoes and Red Cabbage.

**Venison Steaks with Blackberry Wine Sauce**

Venison steaks are quickly pan-seared and served with a delicious blackberry sauce

INGREDIENTS:

4 venison steaks (average weight 8 to 10 ounces each)

2 tablespoons shallot, minced

1 teaspoon minced garlic

4 tablespoons blackberry jam

1 cup red wine

1 cup beef stock

1 tablespoon butter

Salt and ground black pepper to taste

1 pint fresh blackberries

DIRECTIONS:

Heat shallots, garlic, blackberry jam, and red wine in a saucepan over medium-high heat.

Simmer, stirring frequently for about 15 minutes.

Strain the liquid through a fine mesh sieve and set aside.

Heat the beef broth in a separate skillet over medium-high heat until reduced by half, 15 to 20 minutes.

Whisk the two reduced sauces together and stir in the butter.

Season with salt and pepper.

Heat a skillet over medium-high heat.

Cook the venison steaks until they are beginning to firm, and are hot and slightly pink in the center, 3 to 4 minutes per side.

An instant-read thermometer inserted into the center should read at least 145 degrees F (65 degrees C).

Serve the steaks with the sauce and add blackberries as an edible garnish.

**Million Dollar Stew**

1 to 2 pounds venison

2 cans cream of mushroom soup

1 envelope dry Lipton's onion-mushroom soup mix

4-5 skinned & cubed potatoes

1 Cup of water

Cut meat into bite size chunks and place in crock pot.

Add cubed potatoes and cover with cream of mushroom soup.

Sprinkle dry onion-mushroom soup mix on top and add cup of water.

Cook on low or medium overnight (approximately eight hours).

Venison should fall apart when done.

## Venison Medallions with Mushrooms

1 pound venison tenderloin, cut in medallions

Salt

Pepper

1 large onion, sliced thin

2 cloves garlic, diced fine

3 Tbsp. butter

6 ounces mushrooms

1½ Tbsp. flour

1 cup water (you can also use 50/50 dry sherry and water)

1 beef bouillon cube


Sprinkle salt and pepper over venison and put it aside.

In a large non-stick pan, sauté the onions in 1 tablespoon of butter until are partially done; add garlic and cook another 2 or 3 minutes; add mushrooms and sauté another 5 or 10 minutes.

While the vegetables are cooking, use another skillet, either stainless or cast iron (that can be put in a 400 degree oven) for the venison.

Put 1 tablespoon butter in the pan and quickly brown both sides of the venison then put the pan in a 400 degree oven for about 5 minutes, depending upon thickness.

While the venison cooks, add 1 tablespoon butter and the flour to the vegetable pan, stirring until it becomes a paste.

Add the liquid and continue to stir until it develops a gravy consistency.

Remove the medallions and let rest for 3–5 minutes.

Serve vegetables and sauce over the medallions.

**Venison Niçoise Salad**

1 venison steak, sliced

Garlic

Salt

Pepper

Romaine lettuce

Hardboiled eggs, sliced

Red potatoes

Green beans

Cherry tomatoes

Grilled red and yellow peppers

Black olives

Green olives

Blue-cheese

Salad Dressing

Prepare the steak with garlic, salt, and pepper.

Allow the steak to cool.

Thinly slice the steak.

Arrange sliced steak on a serving platter with all of the other ingredients.

All ingredients should be cooked or prepared before arranging the serving platter.

Finish by lightly sprinkling salt, pepper and salad dressing over all of the ingredients.

Venison Nicoise Salad

## Tasty Oriental Venison Noodles

1 tbsp. canola oil

3 cloves chopped garlic

1 tsp. minced ginger (fresh or dried)

1/4 tsp. crushed red pepper

1 sweet onion, chopped

1 lb. ground venison

1/3 cup sweet chili sauce

1/4 cup reduced sodium soy sauce

1/2 cup beef broth

2 T. cornstarch

¼ cup beef broth

2 tbsp. dry sherry

1 pkg. Soba noodles, cooked according to package directions

1 tbsp. toasted sesame oil

1/4 cup sliced green onions


Heat large skillet until hot; add the oil, garlic, ginger, onion and pepper flakes.

Stir and sauté.

Add in the ground meat and stir frequently while the meat browns.

In a small bowl combine the beef broth, chili sauce and soy sauce.  Stir this mixture into the meat mixture.

Reduce heat, cover and allow to simmer for about ten minutes.

Add onion and ground meat; cook, stirring frequently until meat is browned.

In a small bowl, combine, chili sauce, soy sauce and beef broth.

Stir into meat mixture.

Cover; reduce heat and simmer 10 minutes.

Meanwhile, dissolve cornstarch in remaining beef broth. Add dry sherry.

Stir into meat mixture; cook and stir until the sauce is thick.

In a separate bowl, combine the cooked noodles and sesame oil, stir and add venison mixture.

Toss to combine then sprinkle with the green onions.

## Pan-Seared Cherry Venison

This is a wonderful fall and winter dish. The addition of the tart cherries really creates a special dish.

1 1/2 teaspoons chopped fresh rosemary

1 teaspoon coriander seeds

2 large garlic cloves

1 shallot

1 1/2 teaspoons olive oil

1 tablespoon butter

1 (1-lb) venison tenderloin

1/3 cup dry red wine

1/4 cup dried tart cherries

1 cup beef broth

1/4 cup water

1 teaspoon cornstarch

2 tablespoons jelly

Salt and pepper


Grind 1 teaspoon rosemary with coriander seeds and garlic with a mortar and pestle to make a paste, then stir in 1/2 teaspoon oil.


Pat venison dry and put in a bowl, then rub with paste. Season well with pepper, then cover and chill 20 minutes.

Heat a well-seasoned cast-iron skillet over high heat until hot, then add remaining teaspoon oil, tilting skillet to coat evenly.

Season venison well with salt and pepper, then brown, turning once, about six minutes total.

Reduce heat and cover venison. Allow to cook until venison reaches 125 degrees.

Transfer meat to a plate and cover tightly with foil.

Add butter and shallots to the skillet and cook for 30 seconds.

Add wine and cherries to skillet and deglaze by boiling over moderately high heat, stirring and scraping up brown bits.

Stir together broth, water, cornstarch, and remaining rosemary in a bowl and add to skillet.

Simmer, stirring, until mixture is thickened, about five minutes.

Whisk in jelly and salt and pepper to taste.

Cut venison into 1/4-inch-thick slices and serve with sauce.

**Venison Panini**

This hearty Panini is sure to be a crowd pleasing favorite.


Venison tenderloin

Wholegrain bread, sliced (two slices per sandwich)

Apple, sliced (I like Granny Smith the best as it adds that nice tartness to the combination. You'll want one apple for every two sandwiches)

Cinnamon

Sugar

Sharp cheddar cheese, sliced 2 slices per sandwich

Butter (softened)


Dry Rub:

Ginger

Nutmeg

Salt

Pepper


Coat tenderloin with dry rub.

Preheat grill, then grill tenderloin at highest possible temperature.

Cook until slightly rare and remove tenderloin from heat.

Brush butter onto one side of each slice of bread.

Sprinkle cinnamon and sugar onto sliced apples and stir. Slice venison into thin pieces.

Place a few venison slices on the unbuttered side of a slice of bread.

Add a few apples and slices of cheese.

Top with another slice of bread, butter side up.

Place sandwiches on grill and cook on low heat.

Place weight on the sandwiches using a Panini press.

Flip sandwich once one side is toasted.

There is a nice Panini maker available in stores like Wal-Mart. If you have a Panini Maker you can use it versus the method above.

Serve and enjoy.

## Venison and Gorgonzola Puff Pastry

This is a hearty combination nicely balanced with the puff pastry.

1 lb. ground venison

1/4 tsp. salt

1/4 tsp. black pepper

2 tablespoons prepared horseradish

1 sm. onion, chopped

1 egg, beaten

1 sheet frozen puff pastry, defrosted

Crumbled Gorgonzola cheese (or other favorite cheese)


Sauté venison with onion and spices.

Add horseradish. Remove from heat to cool slightly.

Add the cheese.  I tend to go heavy on the cheese but you can add as much or little as you see fit.

Follow package instructions for preparing pastry sheet.

Place the sheet on a baking pan covered with parchment paper.

Put filling on one half of the sheet.

Fold over pastry sheet and crimp edges with fork to seal.

Make a couple small slits on the top, and brush top with beaten egg.

Bake at 400 degrees for 20-30 minutes, or until top is browned and puffed.

**Pecan Venison**

4 or more venison steaks (preferably from the backstrap)

1 tbsp. olive oil

1 tsp. minced garlic

1 cup sliced onion

8 ounces sliced mushrooms

3 tbsp. medium dry sherry

2 cups vegetable broth

½ cup heavy cream

2 tsp. cornstarch

1/3 cup pecan halves

¼ cup green onions, finely sliced

Season the venison with salt and pepper.

Heat olive oil in a non-stick skillet, add venison and cook until venison is rare.

Remove from skillet.

Add onion and mushrooms to pan; cook 3 to 5 minutes.

Add garlic and cook 2 more minutes.

Add sherry and cook 1 minute.

Add broth and boil until liquid is reduced by half, skimming any fat or foam.

Combine 2 tbsp. cream with the cornstarch.

Add remaining cream to skillet and bring to a gentle boil.

Whisk in the cornstarch mixture, simmer 4 to 5 minutes.  Stir frequently.

Add venison, pecans and green onion.

Simmer about 2 minutes and serve.

**Venison Pot Roast**

This dish is perfect for Sunday dinner or any time you want to enjoy a classic and hearty meal.

2 ½ to 3 lb. venison roast

1/3 cup flour

½ tsp. marjoram leaves

½ tsp. thyme

½ tsp. garlic salt

¼ tsp. pepper

1 can French onion soup

½ cup coffee

3 Tbsp. cooking oil

4 small turnips

1 small bag mini carrots

2 stalks of celery, cut up

2 medium onions, quartered


Preheat oven to 350°F.

Combine first five ingredients in a large plastic bag and mix.

Add the roast and shake to coat.

Brown the roast on all sides in cooking oil in a Dutch oven.

Add the rest of the flour mixture, the soup and the coffee and stir until smooth and bubbly.

Cover and bake for 1 to 1½ hours.

Add the vegetables and return to oven.

Bake for another 1 to 1½ hours, until meat and vegetables are tender.

Leftovers make great sandwiches too.

Thank you for taking the time to purchase and read Best Venison Recipes Volume 1

Printed in Great Britain
by Amazon

22459564R00064